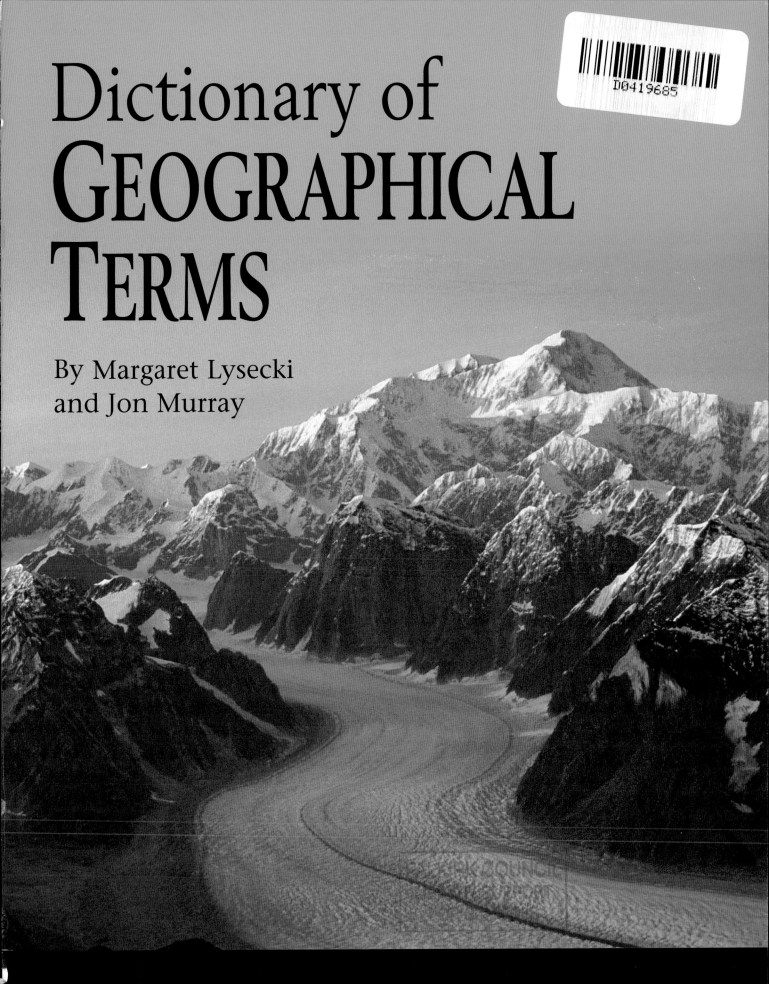

Dictionary of
GEOGRAPHICAL
TERMS

By Margaret Lysecki
and Jon Murray

Series Literacy Consultant
Dr Ros Fisher

Pearson Education Limited
Edinburgh Gate
Harlow
Essex CM20 2JE
England

www.longman.co.uk

The rights of Margaret Lysecki and Jon Murray to be identified as the authors of this Work have been asserted by them in accordance with the Copyright, Designs and Patents Act, 1988.

ISBN 0 582 84549 1

Colour reproduction by Colourscan, Singapore
Printed and bound in China by Leo Paper Products Ltd.

The Publisher's policy is to use paper manufactured from sustainable forests.

The following people from **DK** have
contributed to the development of this product:

Art Director Rachael Foster

Keith Davis, Carole Oliver **Design** | **Managing Editor** Scarlett O'Hara
Carlo Ortu **Picture Research** | **Editorial** Ben Hoare, Kate Pearce
Ed Merritt **Cartography** | **Production** Rosalind Holmes
Richard Czapnik, Andy Smith **Cover Design** | **DTP** David McDonald
Consultant David Green

Dorling Kindersley would like to thank: Johnny Pau for additional cover design work.

Contents

What Is Geography?

The word *geography* comes from ancient Greece. The root *geo* means "Earth". The root *graph* means "writing".

In geography, you study many things. You learn about the Earth's land and water and its climate and weather. You also learn where people live and how groups of people interact with the environment. Geography also teaches us about environmental changes, and the issues and problems these changes present.

There are special words or terms that are used to understand geography. This dictionary will explain what some of those words mean. It will also help you to spell and pronounce the words.

rainforest

hurricane

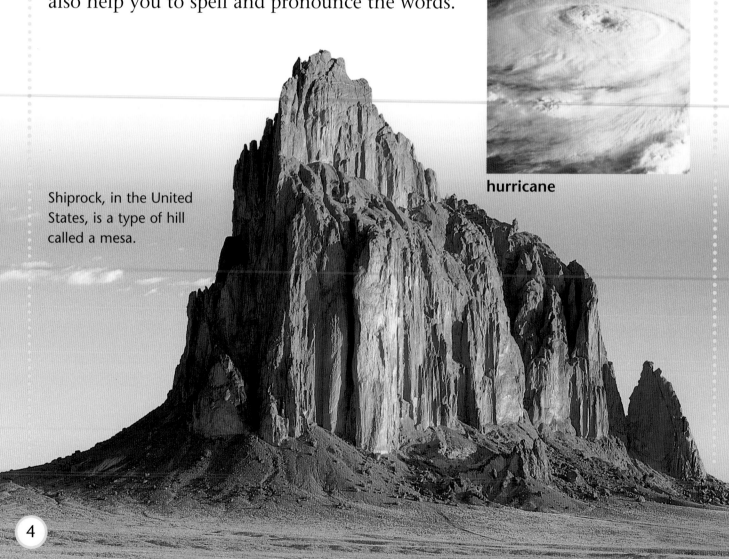

Shiprock, in the United States, is a type of hill called a mesa.

Using the Dictionary

On each page of this dictionary, you will see entry words listed in alphabetical order. Each entry word has a definition. Next to each entry word, in brackets, is its pronunciation. When you read the pronunciation out loud, you will learn how to say the entry word correctly.

At the top of each page you will see two guide words. They are the first and last entry words on the page. Any word that comes in alphabetical order between the guide words may be on the page.

guide words

alphabet

entry word

definition

pronunciation

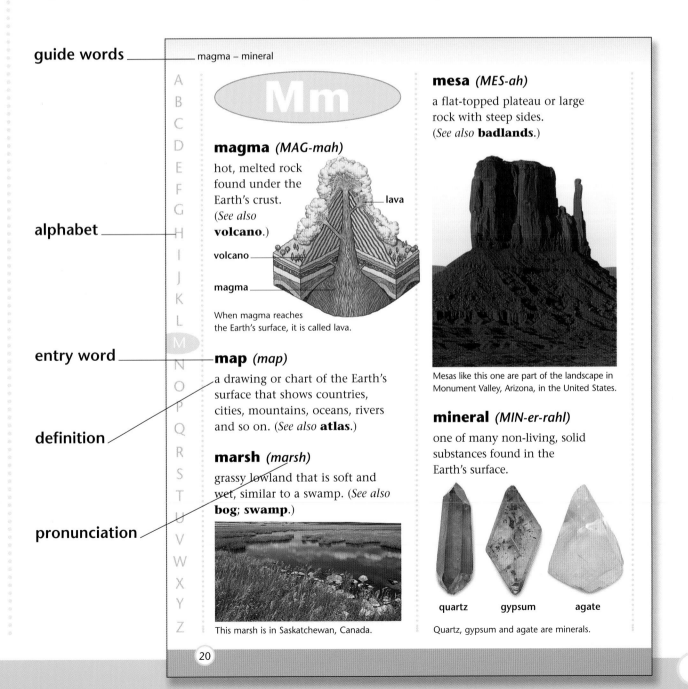

magma – mineral

Mm

magma *(MAG-mah)*
hot, melted rock found under the Earth's crust. *(See also* **volcano**.*)*

lava

volcano

magma

When magma reaches the Earth's surface, it is called lava.

map *(map)*
a drawing or chart of the Earth's surface that shows countries, cities, mountains, oceans, rivers and so on. *(See also* **atlas**.*)*

marsh *(marsh)*
grassy lowland that is soft and wet, similar to a swamp. *(See also* **bog**; **swamp**.*)*

This marsh is in Saskatchewan, Canada.

mesa *(MES-ah)*
a flat-topped plateau or large rock with steep sides. *(See also* **badlands**.*)*

Mesas like this one are part of the landscape in Monument Valley, Arizona, in the United States.

mineral *(MIN-er-rahl)*
one of many non-living, solid substances found in the Earth's surface.

quartz   gypsum   agate

Quartz, gypsum and agate are minerals.

20

Aa

altitude *(AL-tih-tuwd)*

the distance above the Earth's surface. The word is used for objects that are very tall or high up, such as mountains or aeroplanes. (*See also* **elevation**; **sea level**.)

This helicopter and hot-air balloon are at a higher altitude than the mountains.

aqueduct *(AK-wuh-dukt)*

a large pipe or channel used to carry water from one place to another.

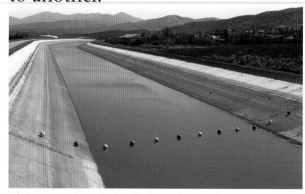

This aqueduct is in California in the United States.

arid *(a-rid)*

dry; a region with little rainfall and not much plant life. (*See also* **desert**; **savannah**.)

atlas *(AT-luss)*

a book of maps. (*See also* **maps**.)

atmosphere *(AT-mus-feer)*

the layer of gases that surrounds the Earth.

outer space

atmosphere

Earth

The atmosphere reaches from the Earth's surface to the start of outer space.

avalanche *(AV-ah-lahnch)*

a large mass of snow, earth or rock that slides quickly downhill. An avalanche can bury anything in its path.

Bb

badlands *(BAD-landz)*

a dry region where rocks have been worn away to form sharp ridges, peaks, cliffs and flat-topped mesas. (*See also* **mesa**.)

barrier island
(BA-ree-er EYE-land)

a long, thin, sandy island that lies a short distance away from the main coastline. The barrier island protects the coastline from strong waves and currents.

This barrier island lies just off the coast of Tahiti in the Pacific Ocean.

barrier reef *(BA-ree-er reef)*

a long, narrow, underwater ridge that is made up of coral, the skeletons of tiny sea animals. It is separated from land by deeper water called a lagoon.

This diagram shows how a barrier reef is separated from the land.

bay *(bay)*

a body of salt water that is connected to the sea or ocean, but is surrounded on three sides by land. (*See also* **inlet**.)

Hudson Bay, Canada, is one of the largest bays in the world.

A B C D E F G H I J K L M N O P Q R S T U V W X Y Z

7

A
B
C
D
E
F
G
H
I
J
K
L
M
N
O
P
Q
R
S
T
U
V
W
X
Y
Z

bayou (BY-yoo)

a slow-moving body of water that leads into or out of a lake or a river. *Bayou* is a term used in the south eastern United States.

beach (beech)

an area of sand and small stones at the edge of a lake, an ocean or another body of water.

This is a sandy beach in Western Australia.

bog (bog)

wet, spongy ground. (*See also* **marsh**; **swamp**.)

Bogs, like this one at Rannoch in Scotland, are wet and muddy places.

border (BOR-dur)

the line that divides one country or state from another country or state. Some borders are natural, such as rivers or mountains. Other borders can only be seen on a map.

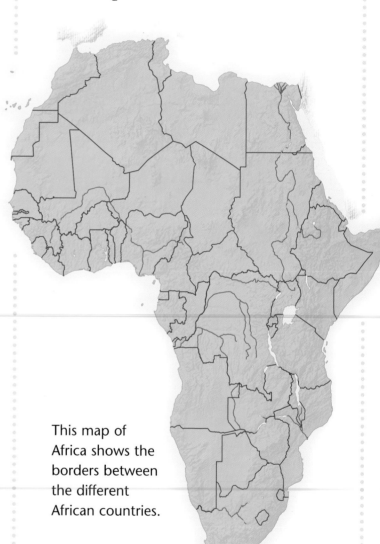

This map of Africa shows the borders between the different African countries.

boundary (BOWN-dah-ree)

the line that marks the outside edge of an area. *Boundary* usually refers to the edge of an area smaller than a country or a state.

A
B
C
D
E
F
G
H
I
J
K
L
M
N
O
P
Q
R
S
T
U
V
W
X
Y
Z

channel *(CHAN-uhl)*

a narrow body of water joining two larger bodies of water.

chasm *(KAZ-uhm)*

a great crack in the Earth, such as a valley, a gorge or a canyon.

city *(sit-ee)*

a large, important town where many people live and work.

cliff *(klif)*

a steep and often high slope of rock or soil.

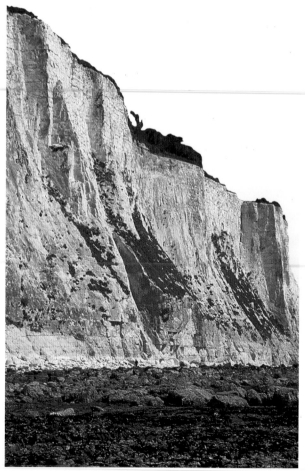

White Cliffs of Dover, England

climate *(KLY-mat)*

the pattern of weather conditions experienced in a place or region over many years.

coast *(kohst)*

the place where land meets a sea or ocean.

This photograph shows the Gold Coast along Queensland, Australia.

compass *(KUM-pus)*

an instrument used to show directions.

compass

Which Way?

The Earth is a large magnet. The needle on a compass is also a magnet. It is pulled by the Earth's magnetism to point towards the North Pole. By reading the needle on a compass, a traveller can find the four major directions: north, south, east and west.

conservation
(KON-sur-vay-shun)

the care, protection and wise use of the environment and other resources.

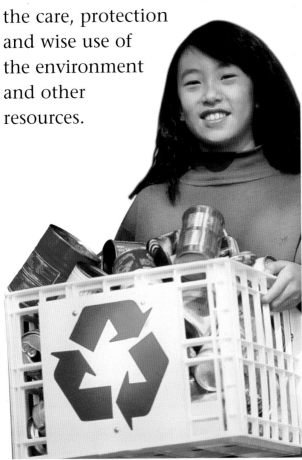

Recycling metal tins and cans is an example of conservation.

continent (KON-tih-nunt)

one of the Earth's seven large masses of land.

The Earth has seven continents.

cordillera (kor-dil-LAIR-uh)

a very large chain of mountains or mountain ranges. It is sometimes the main mountain range of a country or continent.

The Dolomites cordillera is in northern Italy.

cyclone (SY-klone)

a very strong storm with powerful winds that move in a circle around a centre of low pressure. When it occurs in the Indian Ocean region, it is known as a tropical cyclone. (*See also* **hurricane**; **typhoon**.)

This satellite photograph shows a tropical cyclone off the east coast of Madagascar.

Dd

delta (DEL-tah)

a build-up of clay, sand and other deposits at the mouth of a river. A delta is shaped like a triangle.

This photograph shows the Nile Delta in Egypt.

desert (DEH-zert)

a region where very little rain falls. (*See also* **arid**.)

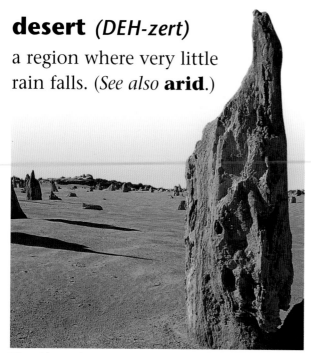

The Pinnacles Desert in Western Australia is named for its strange rock formations.

Many Kinds of Deserts

Deserts may be sandy, like the Sahara Desert in Africa, or rocky, like the Mojave Desert in the United States. Deserts can also be covered in ice and snow, such as the continent Antarctica.

Polar deserts are very dry places in the Arctic, as seen here, and in the Antarctic.

drought (drowt)

a long period of little or no rainfall.

This reservoir in California in the United States has dried up because of a severe drought.

Ee

earthquake *(URTH-kwayk)*

a shaking of the Earth's surface.

In 1989, a powerful earthquake damaged many buildings in San Francisco, California, in the United States.

More About Earthquakes

An earthquake is caused by changes that take place below the surface of the Earth. Large areas of rock, called plates, shift or move. This shifting causes the Earth's surface to shake. Earthquakes may be very mild or very destructive.

shifting plates

centre of earthquake

ecology *(ee-KOL-oh-jee)*

the study of how living things are connected to each other and to their environment.

ecosystem *(EE-koh-sis-tuhm)*

a system of living things and their environment. In an ecosystem, all the living things affect each other.

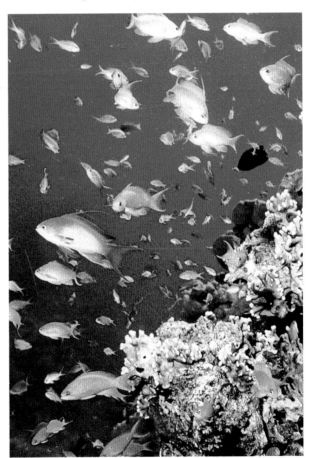

A coral reef is an ecosystem. It is home to colourful corals, fish and other animals.

elevation *(el-er-VAY-shun)*

the height of a landform or an object above sea level. (*See also* **altitude**; **sea level**.)

A
B
C
D
E
F
G
H
I
J
K
L
M
N
O
P
Q
R
S
T
U
V
W
X
Y
Z

environment
(en-VY-ruh-ment)

the physical setting in which plants, animals and humans live and interact.

equator *(e-KWAY-tur)*

an imaginary line around the middle of the Earth. The equator divides the Earth into the northern and southern hemispheres. (*See also* **hemisphere**.)

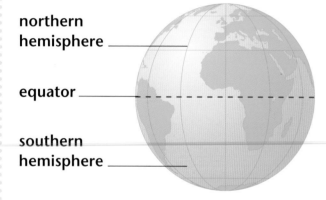

northern hemisphere

equator

southern hemisphere

erosion *(e-ROH-shun)*

the gradual wearing away of the Earth's surface.

Erosion formed this arch in Utah in the United States. The rock was worn away by water.

Many Processes of Erosion

The Earth's surface can be worn away, or eroded, by different processes. Wind and water are the most common causes of erosion. Gravity, waves, glaciers and human actions are other processes that can erode the Earth's surface.

fjord *(fee-awd)*

a long, deep inlet of the sea with steep, mountainous sides or cliffs. Fjords were formed by glaciers.

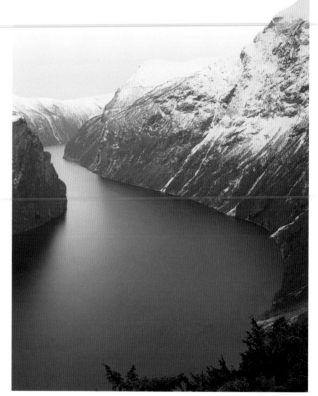

Fjords are very deep and make excellent shelters for ships. This fjord is in Norway.

Gg

geyser *(GEE-zur)*

a spring under the ground that shoots streams of hot water and steam high into the air.

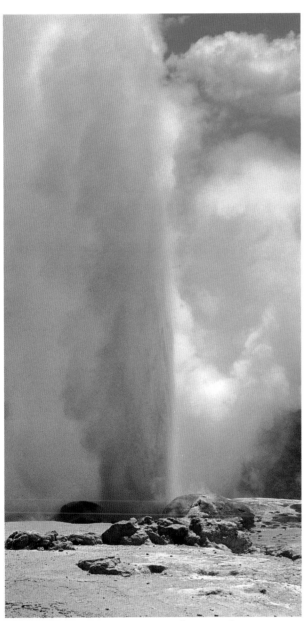

Boiling water and steam rush out of Pohutu Geyser in New Zealand.

glacier *(GLAS-ee-er)*

a large mass of ice that slowly moves downhill.

This massive glacier is in Alberta, Canada.

global warming *(GLOH-buhl WAR-ming)*

an increase in the average temperature of the Earth's atmosphere. It may be caused by the burning of coal, oil and gas, which worsens the greenhouse effect. (*See also* **greenhouse effect**.)

globe *(glohb)*

a round model of the Earth showing continents, countries, oceans and other features.

globe

15

gorge *(gawj)*

a narrow gap between hills or steep rocks, often with a river flowing through it. (*See also* **canyon**.)

The Gorge du Verdon is in southern France.

grassland *(GRAHS-land)*

a wide area of grass-covered land, where few trees grow. Animals often graze there. (*See also* **prairie**; **savannah**.)

Grassland is home to many grazing animals, such as these zebras and impalas in Africa.

greenhouse effect *(GREEN-hows E-fekt)*

a warming process that occurs when certain gases in the atmosphere trap the Sun's heat for long periods of time. (*See also* **global warming**.)

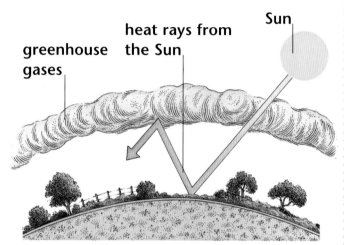

Some gases, called greenhouse gases, trap heat from the Sun close to Earth. This heat warms the Earth.

grid *(grid)*

a pattern of lines that criss-cross, forming squares on a globe or map. They are used to help find locations or features on maps and globes. (*See also* **latitude**; **longitude**.)

Grid lines are often marked on maps.

grid

Hh

habitat *(HAB-ih-tat)*

the environment or area where an animal or plant lives.

A pond is a common habitat for frogs.

hemisphere *(HEM-is-feer)*

any of the halves of the Earth. The equator is an imaginary line that divides the Earth into the northern and southern hemispheres. The prime meridian is an imaginary line that divides the Earth into the eastern and western hemispheres.

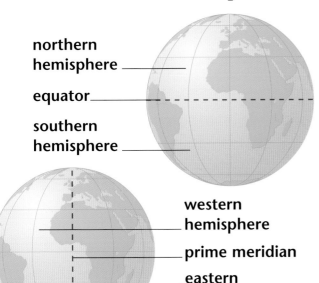

northern hemisphere

equator

southern hemisphere

western hemisphere

prime meridian

eastern hemisphere

humidity *(hyoo-MID-uh-tee)*

the amount of water vapour in the atmosphere. Warm air holds more moisture than cool air. Therefore, warm air can be more humid. As warm air rises, the moisture it contains forms droplets which join together to create clouds.

Clouds are a kind of water vapour.

hurricane *(HUR-rih-kayn)*

a powerful tropical storm with very high winds. It usually includes heavy rains, thunder and lightning. Hurricanes usually start in the Atlantic Ocean or the Caribbean Sea. (*See also* **cyclone**; **typhoon**.)

During a hurricane, winds blow at over 117 kilometres per hour.

A B C D E F G H I J K L M N O P Q R S T U V W X Y Z

inlet *(IN-let)*

a small bay or stream that runs inland from an ocean or a river. (*See also* **bay**.)

The coast of Scotland has many inlets.

irrigation *(ihr-e-gay-shun)*

the use of pipes, ditches or streams to bring water to land for farming.

An irrigation system is used to help these crops grow in Hanalei Valley, Hawaii, in the United States.

island *(EYE-land)*

an area of land, smaller than a continent, that is surrounded on all sides by water.

key *(kee)*

a list that explains the symbols on a map or chart. The symbols stand for actual places or objects.

Map Key

——	State boundary
20	Interstate highway
76	US route
★	State capital
⊙	Other city

A key can help you to read this map of the state of Georgia in the United States.

lake *(layk)*

a large body of fresh or salt water that is often surrounded by land.

This lake is in the Northwest Territories of Canada.

landform *(LAND-form)*

a shape or structure that is formed naturally on the surface of the Earth. A mountain is one example of a landform.

The Bungle Bungles in Western Australia are an example of a landform.

landslide *(LAND-slyd)*

a mass of soil and rocks that moves quickly down a hill. It can be caused by an earthquake, heavy rain, or the cutting away of the base of a slope.

This landslide in Turkey damaged a road.

latitude *(LAT-ih-tuwd)*

horizontal grid lines on a map or a globe. Latitude is used to show location north or south of the equator and is measured in degrees.

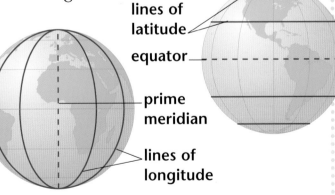

lines of latitude
equator
prime meridian
lines of longitude

longitude *(LONG-ih-tuwd)*

vertical grid lines on a map or a globe. Longitude is used to show location east or west of the prime meridian and is measured in degrees.

A B C D E F G H I J K L M N O P Q R S T U V W X Y Z

19

Mm

magma (MAG-mah)

hot, melted rock found under the Earth's crust. (*See also* **volcano**.)

When magma reaches the Earth's surface, it is called lava.

map (map)

a drawing or chart of the Earth's surface that shows countries, cities, mountains, oceans, rivers and so on. (*See also* **atlas**.)

marsh (marsh)

grassy lowland that is soft and wet, similar to a swamp. (*See also* **bog**; **swamp**.)

This marsh is in Saskatchewan, Canada.

mesa (MES-ah)

a flat-topped plateau or large rock with steep sides. (*See also* **badlands**.)

Mesas like this one are part of the landscape in Monument Valley, Arizona, in the United States.

mineral (MIN-er-rahl)

one of many non-living, solid substances found in the Earth's surface.

quartz   gypsum   agate

Quartz, gypsum and agate are minerals.

monolith *(MON-uh-lith)*

a huge block of stone, such as Uluru in Australia's Northern Territory.

Uluru lies near the centre of the Australian continent. It is over 9 km around its base.

monsoon *(MON-soon)*

a wind that occurs mainly in the Indian Ocean region and southern Asia. It usually blows from the south west in summer and from the north east in winter.

moor *(maw)*

an area of rolling land that is often covered with heather. Moors can be dry or marshy.

mountain *(MOWN-tin)*

a landform that rises above its surroundings.

The Matterhorn in Switzerland is one of Europe's tallest mountains.

Nn

nation *(NAY-shun)*

a large community of people living in the same country under the same government.

natural resource *(NACH-uhr-uhl RI-sors)*

a material found in nature that can be used by people and animals. Water, soil and coal are examples of natural resources. Natural resources may be used to make other things.

kettle   bricks   books

These everyday items are all made from natural resources.

non-renewable resource *(non-ree-new-uh-buhl RI-sors)*

a raw material that is limited in supply. Once it is used up, it cannot be replaced. Crude oil is a non-renewable resource.

North Pole *(north pohl)*

the place that is furthest north on the Earth.

A B C D E F G H I J K L M N O P Q R S T U V W X Y Z

Oo

Pp

ocean *(o-shun)*

the large body of salt water that covers three-quarters of the Earth's surface. The ocean is all connected, but it is divided into several major areas, including the Atlantic, Pacific and Indian Oceans.

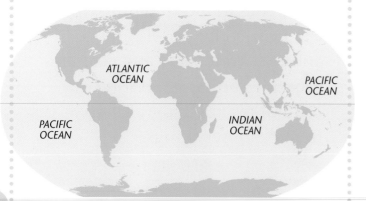

The Earth's ocean is divided into several major areas. Some of them are shown on this map.

The ocean provides us with many things, including food and minerals.

peninsula *(puh-NIN-syoo-lah)*

a piece of land surrounded on three sides by water, or that extends out into a body of water.

The Arabian Peninsula is enclosed by the Red Sea, the Indian Ocean and the Persian Gulf.

plain *(playn)*

a large area of flat or almost flat land. (*See also* **prairie**.)

Plains are often good for growing crops. These fields are in Israel.

plateau (PLA-tow)

a large, raised landform that is fairly flat or level on top.

This plateau in Arizona in the United States is surrounded by cliffs.

polar climate
(POH-lar KLY-maht)

a climate that occurs in the areas of the North Pole and the South Pole.

Polar climates are extremely cold.

pollution (pol-LOO-shun)

the dirtying of land, water or air with harmful substances or materials.

pond (pond)

a small body of water. It is either formed naturally or made artificially, such as a pond in a garden.

population
(pop-yoo-LAY-shun)

the total number of people living in an area or country.

China has the world's largest population. This street is in the Chinese city of Shanghai.

Population Table	
China	1,284,304,000
India	1,045,845,000
United States	287,041,000
Indonesia	232,072,000
Brazil	176,030,000
Pakistan	147,663,000
Russia	144,979,000
Bangladesh	133,377,000
Nigeria	129,935,000
Japan	126,975,000
Mexico	103,400,000
Philippines	84,526,000
United Kingdom	59,778,000
Canada	31,902,000
Australia	19,547,000

prairie (PRAIR-ee)

a large, mostly flat, grass-covered area with few or no trees.

A
B
C
D
E
F
G
H
I
J
K
L
M
N
O
P
Q
R
S
T
U
V
W
X
Y
Z

precipitation
(pre-sip-it-a-shun)

water droplets or ice crystals that fall from the atmosphere to the ground. Precipitation can fall as mist, drizzle, rain, sleet, hail or snow.

prime meridian
(prym mer-RIH-dee-uhn)

the line of longitude at 0° that separates the eastern hemisphere from the western hemisphere. (*See also* **hemisphere**; **longitude**.)

prime meridian _____

promontory
(PROM-uhn-tree)

a high ridge of land or rock that sticks out into a body of water.

The Cape of Good Hope is a promontory at the southern tip of the African continent.

province (PROV-ins)

a district or part of a country. It has its own government to decide local matters, but it also answers to the central government of the country. (*See also* **state**.)

provincial city
(proh-VIN-shul sit-ee)

a city located outside the main population area of a state. A provincial city is the centre of a region and provides services to people who live within and near its boundaries.

Qq

quarry (KWOHR-ee)

a place where rock or stone that is used for building material is blasted or cut out of the Earth.

This quarry in Wales is 305 metres deep.

rainforest *(rayn FOHR-est)*

an area that is densely forested with tall trees and other vegetation. Rainforests have heavy rainfall throughout the year. Most rainforests are found near the equator. They are home to more kinds of plants and animals than any other environment on Earth.

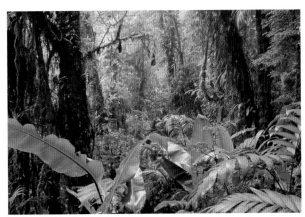

Thick vegetation grows in rainforests, like this one in Costa Rica.

range *(raynj)*

a row of connected hills or mountains.

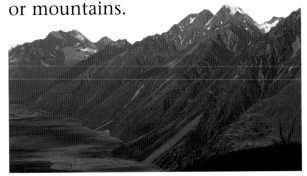

The Southern Alps is a mountain range on the South Island of New Zealand.

reservation *(rez-ur-VAY-shun)*

an area of public land that is set aside for the use of native peoples.

river *(RIV-er)*

a large, natural stream of water that flows into another river, a lake or an ocean.

river

river's source

ocean

This diagram shows how a river flows down to an ocean.

rural *(ROOR-uhl)*

having to do with areas that are mainly countryside with sparse populations. Farming is often important in these areas. (*See also* **population**; **urban**.)

This photograph shows cows grazing in a rural area in Devon, England.

savannah *(suh-VAN-ah)*

a grassy plain with a scattering of trees and seasonal rainfall. It is found in places with a tropical or subtropical climate. (*See also* **grassland; prairie**.)

This picture shows a savannah in Africa.

sea *(see)*

a large body of water, usually salt water, that is partly surrounded by land.

sea level *(see LEH-vul)*

the height of the surface of the ocean. Sea level is used to measure the height of an area or a landform. A mountain might be hundreds of metres above sea level; a canyon hundreds of metres below sea level.

settlement *(SEH-tul-munt)*

any place to which people have moved to live. Settlements can be large or small, and new or old.

This settlement is on a hillside in Caracas, the capital city of Venezuela, in South America.

South Pole *(sowth pohl)*

the place that is furthest south on Earth.

state *(stayt)*

an area of land whose people have their own government. In the United States, states share power with the federal government. (*See also* **province**.)

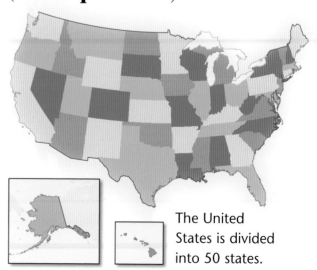

The United States is divided into 50 states.

strait (strayt)

a narrow waterway that connects two larger bodies of water.

The Strait of Gibraltar connects the Atlantic Ocean with the Mediterranean Sea.

stream (streem)

a small body of flowing water, such as a brook or a creek.

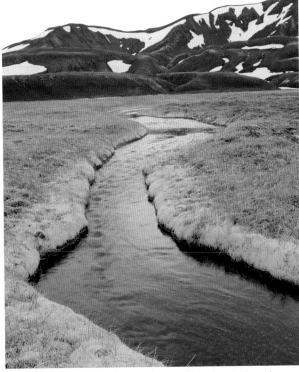

This stream runs through a valley in Iceland.

suburb (sub-erb)

an area of homes and small businesses that is immediately outside a city.

This suburb is outside Las Vegas, Nevada, in the United States.

summit (SUM-it)

the top or highest place of a hill or a mountain.

swamp (swomp)

a wet, soft lowland with trees and plants. (*See also* **bog**; **marsh**.)

This swamp is in Papua New Guinea.

A
B
C
D
E
F
G
H
I
J
K
L
M
N
O
P
Q
R
S
T
U
V
W
X
Y
Z

Tt

temperate climate
(TEM-pah-riht KLY-mat)

a climate zone that has mild seasons, including warm summers and cool or cold winters. (*See also* **climate**.)

timber line (TIM-bur-lyne)

the height on a mountain above which trees will not grow due to the harsh climate. Also, the timber line, or tree line, is the distance north or south of the equator beyond which trees will not grow. (*See also* **equator**.)

These Canadian mountains are forested below the timber line and bare above it.

tornado (tohr-NAY-dow)

a small, violent windstorm with a funnel-shaped cloud. Tornadoes are very destructive.

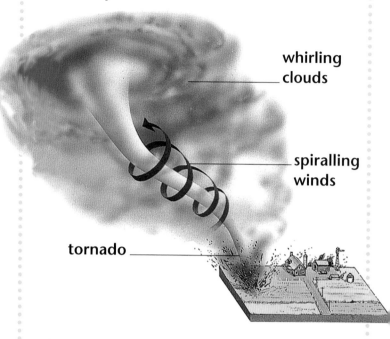

whirling clouds

spiralling winds

tornado

tributary
(TRIB-yoo-tair-ee)

a stream or river that flows into a larger stream or river.

The tributary on the left joins a much larger river on the right.

Tropic of Cancer
(TROP-ik of KAN-sur)

an imaginary circle around the Earth. This line is 23.5° north of the equator and is parallel to it.

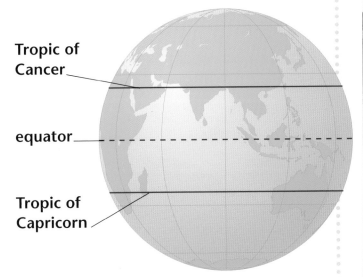

Tropic of Capricorn
(TROP-ik of KAP-ree-korn)

an imaginary circle around the Earth. This line is 23.5° south of the equator and is parallel to it.

tropical climate
(TROP-ik-uhl KLY-mat)

a climate in which it is warm or hot most of the year, with extreme heat and heavy rains in the summer. (*See also* **climate**; **tropics**.)

tropics *(TROP-iks)*

the regions near the equator; the hottest parts of the Earth.

tundra *(TUN-drah)*

a vast, treeless area found in Arctic regions. The tundra is mostly flat. Even in the brief summer, the soil is always frozen a few metres below the surface.

Tundra covers much of Greenland.

typhoon *(ty-FOON)*

a type of tropical storm with high winds and strong rains that forms over the western Pacific Ocean near Asia. (*See also* **cyclone**; **hurricane**.)

Typhoons can cause serious flooding and damage if they reach land.

A B C D E F G H I J K L M N O P Q R S T U V W X Y Z

urban *(UR-buhn)*

having to do with cities. Urban areas have many people, buildings, traffic and businesses.

Sydney and its surrounding areas make up the largest urban region in Australia.

Vv

valley *(VAL-ee)*

an area of low land that lies between two hills or mountains.

This fertile valley is in Killarney, Ireland.

vegetation
(vej-e-tay-shun)

any or all of the plants in a certain area.

volcano *(vol-KAY-no)*

an opening in the Earth's crust where lava, rock, gases and dust are sometimes forced out. (*See also* **magma**.)

Puu Oo spews molten lava on Big Island, Hawaii, in the United States.

A Look At Volcanoes

Volcanoes are found on the ocean floor as well as on land. Mt Pinatubo in the Philippines is an example of a volcano that erupts violently and causes great destruction. Mauna Loa in Hawaii in the United States erupts frequently but usually less violently.

Ww

wetland *(WET-land)*

area of land that contains marshes or swamps. (*See also* **swamp**.)

Climate Map of the World

This map shows the climate, or normal weather conditions, in each
region of the world. Each type of climate is shown in a different colour.

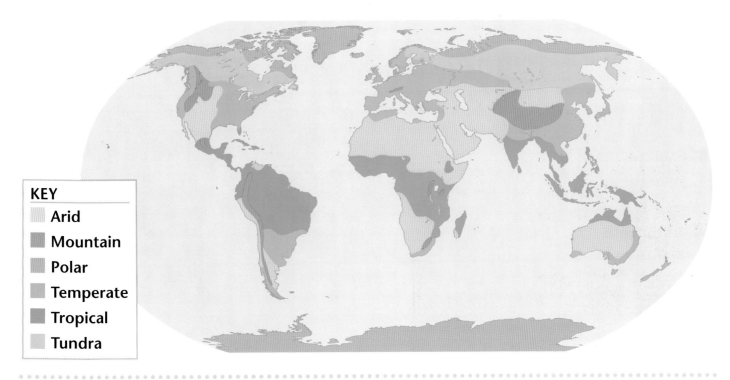

KEY
- Arid
- Mountain
- Polar
- Temperate
- Tropical
- Tundra

Physical Map of the World

On this map, you can see the height of the land in different parts
of the world.

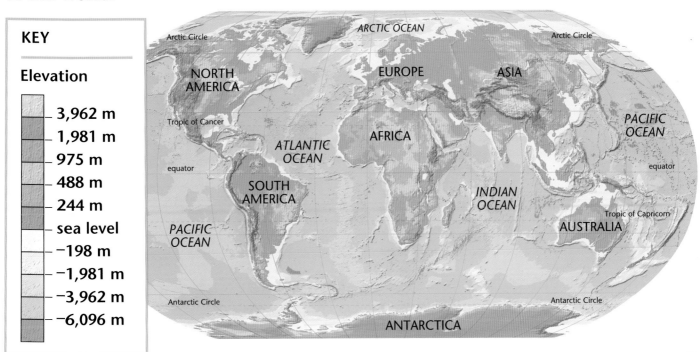

KEY

Elevation

- 3,962 m
- 1,981 m
- 975 m
- 488 m
- 244 m
- sea level
- −198 m
- −1,981 m
- −3,962 m
- −6,096 m

Language Map of the World

This map shows the main languages spoken around the world.
Each language is shown in a different colour.

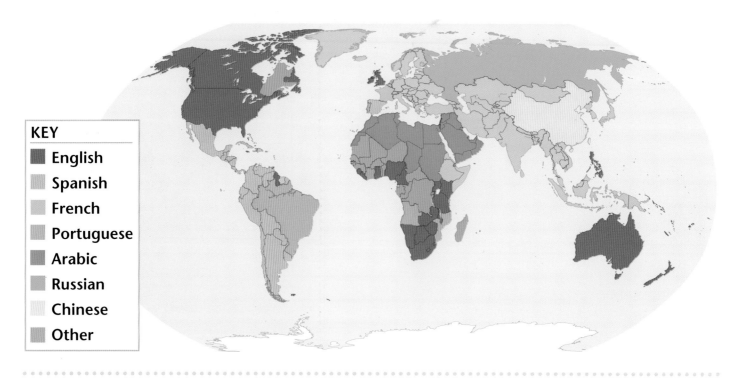

KEY
- English
- Spanish
- French
- Portuguese
- Arabic
- Russian
- Chinese
- Other

Population Map of the World

This map of the world shows the population density, or the number of
people living in each square kilometre.

KEY

People per square km
- More than 260
- 52–259
- 24–51
- Less than 24